THE FIRST WORLD WAR IN PHOTOGRAPHS

1915

JOHN CHRISTOPHER & CAMPBELL McCUTCHEON

AMBERLEY

First published 2014

Amberley Publishing
The Hill, Stroud
Gloucestershire, GL5 4EP

www.amberley-books.com

British Library Cataloguing in Publication Data.
A catalogue record for this book is available from the British Library.

ISBN 978 1 4456 2205 7 (print)
ISBN 978 1 4456 2221 7 (ebook)

Typeset in 11pt on 15pt Sabon.
Typesetting and Origination by Amberley Publishing.
Printed in the UK.

Contents

A German patrol on the Western Front in the summer of 1915.

Introduction –
The year of no warnings

For a fight that would be over by Christmas 1914, New Year 1915 saw the world still at war, and a war that had spread even further afield too. Some things had changed – the armies of the world were bogged down in France, in the Caucasus, the Turks were fighting against Russians and on 13 January it was decided in a Council of War that Britain would make a naval attack against Turkey to open the Dardanelles seaway to French and British ships, which could then supply Russia with arms and supplies. Winston Churchill, First Lord of the Admiralty, is chief advocate of the attack. By the 26th, the French have given their approval and plans are set in motion for the new campaign. The Battle of Sarikamish between 1 and 3 January sees the Turks advance on Kars. 95,000 troops under Enver Pasha are suddenly attacked in a Russian counterattack. Retreat ensues with 30,000 Turks dead and the strength of those who retreat numbering only 19,000 fit for service. On 14 January, the Turks advance from Beersheba towards the Suez Canal and on the 19th, Britain is attacked from the air. Zeppelins L3 and L4 cause twenty casualties on their raid on eastern England.

On 24 January there is a sea battle between elements of the British fleet and Admiral Hipper's *Blücher, Derfflinger, Moltke* and *Seydlitz*. After December's shelling of Yorkshire and incessant attacks on the fishing fleet, public opinion wants action against the Germans and Admiral Beatty moves a small fleet to Rosyth from Scapa Flow. Wireless chatter told the Admiralty that Hipper's squadron was on the move and Beatty and Hipper meet on the Dogger Bank. Catching Hipper unawares, despite the Zeppelin and destroyer escort, Beatty's battleships sank the *Blücher* by midday but the *Lion* was damaged by shells from *Derfflinger*. Transferring to *Princess Royal*, Beatty could do little but watch the remaining German ships escape. The poor firing of the British fleet certainly did not help. Only seventy-three hits were recorded from 958 shells fired. Political shenanigans see David Lloyd George suggest to the British War Council that Anglo-French forces are sent to Salonika, Greece, in an attempt to open a new front with Balkan states declaring war on Austria-Hungary. The Greeks reject the offer. On 30 January, U-20 sank two ships without warning in the English Channel. Previously, crews had been given an opportunity to abandon ship. By the end of the month, relations between Austria-Hungary and Italy reach a new low and Austrian forces begin to protect the difficult mountain border between the two erstwhile allies.

January sees the advent of chemical warfare, with the use by the Germans of gas shells on the Eastern Front. Soon, the French and British would develop their own terrible and indiscriminate weapons. Gases used include xylyl bromide, a form of tear gas. Chlorine gas follows but the most deadly gases are phosgene and mustard gas. The mustard gas attacks the lungs, but also the skin too. It could, and did, cause permanent blindness to many on both sides.

Germany's Ninth Army fights its way towards Warsaw. The Battle of Bolimov opens with 600 artillery pieces firing 18,000 xylyl bromide shells towards the Russians. The extreme cold and winds mean the Russians hardly notice the effects of the gas and do not inform their allies of its use. The battle itself sees Russian counterattacks on 6 February, with the loss of 20,000 on each side. However, Bolimov is nothing but a diversionary attack for the main German/Austro-Hungarian advance, which begins on the 7th. Two German armies advance from the Masurian lakes in East Prussia towards Russia. In the Carpathians, the Austro-Hungarians are determined to retake their Galician province, lost in 1914 to the Russians.

Below: Some of the crew of HMS *Ajax* larking around on the fo'c'sle. After the huge expansion of the Royal Navy before the war, the ships spent much time in harbour, where the crews had time on their hands.

Above: Delegates for the 1915 Peace Conference held in The Hague, April 1915. Photographed aboard MS *Noordan*.

In February, the blockade of Germany had begun to have a huge effect and rationing of bread and flour was introduced. Not until 1917 would Britain see similar restrictions. The first of the month sees the German government agree to allow unrestricted submarine warfare against all ships in the war zone around Britain, including neutral vessels. The third sees the Turkish advance on the Suez Canal thwarted by Indian troops. With 2,000 casualties, the Turks retreat to Beersheba. Von Hindenburg begins the pincer attack against the Russians on 7 February. Soon elements of the Russian Tenth Army are surrounded but they fight a brilliant defence, allowing many of their comrades to escape. By the 22nd, some 70 miles have been taken and 90,000 Russians captured. German orders for attacks on Britain by air are finalised by the Kaiser on 12 February, with legitimate targets including military bases and dockyards, but excluding civilian areas and royal palaces. Turkey decides to commit genocide against the Armenians on 14 February. Three days later, the attacks in the East stall due to the atrocious weather. On 19 February, French and British warships begin to bombard the Turkish forts protecting the Dardanelles seaway between the Black Sea and the Mediterranean. Plans are well advanced for the invasion of the Dardanelles from the sea. The Australian and New Zealand troops in Egypt are primed for the attack on the Dardanelles. In Africa, General Louis Botha makes an exploratory raid into German South West Africa on 22 February. Soon 43,000 South African troops

LORD LANSDOWNE, MR. LLOYD GEORGE, MR. WINSTON CHURCHILL,
Minister without Portfolio. Minister of Munitions. Chancellor of the Duchy of Lancaster.

'Prominent members of the Coalition Cabinet.' The original wartime coalition was led by Herbert Asquith. Meanwhile, Lloyd George, as Minister of Munitions, would emerge from the 1915 Shell Crisis as a popular leader and went on to become Prime Minister the following year. Churchill is shown top right. Dismissed as the First Lord of the Admiralty in May 1915 following the failure of the naval attacks in the Dardanelles, he resigned from the government in November.

Above: Men of the Royal Naval Division in training at the Crystal Palace, Sydenham, South London. The Royal Naval Division became a major component of the British Army.

mass against the 9,000 Germans, with the invasion proper beginning on 7 March. In Austria-Hungary food shortages see the government take control of distribution of grain and flour on 24 February.

At the beginning of March, the British announce that they will 'prevent commodities of any kind entering or leaving Germany'. Despite protests from the US, the policy comes into force. The French create the first ever specialized fighter squadron under Commandant baron de Tricornet, with Parasol fighters. On the 6th, the Austro-Hungarians tell the Germans that war with Italy is inevitable. An offensive at Neuve-Chapelle takes place, with the Royal Flying Corps performing much valued spotting work, as well as ground support for the advancing troops. This limited offensive, between 10–13 March, sees 13,500 British casualties but the capture of Neuve-Chapelle itself, as well as some German trenches.

After a three month chase, the SMS *Dresden* is finally located at Juan Fernandez Island, off the coast of Chile, on 14 March. Scuttled by her crew, she is the last of von Spee's East Asiatic Squadron. On 18 March, the last attempts to take the Dardanelles using sea power alone fail. Three ships of Rear Admiral John de Robeck's Anglo-French fleet are sunk by mines with another three damaged. The use of seaplane carriers in the Dardanelles helped solve the problems of lack of airfields. For this *Ark Royal, Ben-my-Chree* and other seaplane carriers were used. Also on 18 March, 21,000 troops attack German South West Africa. The besieged garrison at Przemsyl surrenders and 110,000 Austro-Hungarian troops enter captivity.

Above: Home made bombs aboard HMS *Agamemnon*. With a shortage of bombs, the crew made some out of torpedo warheads and scrap metal, for use against the SMS *Goeben*. In 1916, HMS *Agamemnon* shot down the Zeppelin LZ85 over Salonica. LZ85 crash-landed in marshes outside the city and was brought back to the Vardar quarter of Salonica and the frame rebuilt on the quayside. Scrapped in 1927, *Agamemnon* was the last pre-Dreadnought in the Royal Navy.

Below: Tiger was the eleventh naval vessel to hold the name. After the war, she was the oldest battlecruiser to remain in service and was scrapped in 1932. Her 13.5-in guns could fire two rounds per minute each and she carried 130 rounds per gun. Amidships the armour was nine inches thick.

On 5 April, the French launch an attack against St Mihiel. With poor weather, treacherous mud and a determined German defence, the attack withers and finally dies. The 8th sees the Turks begin their cleansing of Armenia, with the ultimate deaths of over 1 million from the fighting, starvation and disease. Four days later, the Turks are defeated at Shaiba in Mesopotamia by a numerically inferior British force from Basra. The 6,000 British soldiers inflict 3,200 casualties, effectively removing around 30 per cent of the Turks from the fighting. The Kaiser orders the movement of eight divisions from the Western Front to Krakow. It is part of an effort to defeat the Russians so that the war can then concentrate on the gains made in the West.

The first vessel to break through the Turkish defences in the Dardanelles does so on 17 April. The submarine E17 makes the voyage past Turkish forts, mines and anti-submarine nets, causing havoc in the previously safe Black Sea. A breakthrough by Fokker sees the development of the interrupter gear, which allows the firing of a machine gun between the whirling propeller blades of a fighter aircraft. Single seat fighters and dogfights are not far away.

The Second Battle of Ypres begins when the Germans use 4,000 chlorine gas shells and advance. With no protection against the gas, many troops run away, leaving a five mile gap in the front. A second gas attack takes place on the 24th.

The poet Rupert Brooke dies in a French hospital ship off Skyros in Greece on 23 April.

If I should die, think only this of me:
That there's some corner of a foreign field
That is for ever England.

For thousands more, the Greek islands and the beaches and cliffs of the Dardanelles would also be for ever England. The invasion began on the 25th, with British troops landing at Cape Helles and the ANZAC contingent at Ari Burna. French troops land at Kumkale. Stiff Turkish resistance keeps the troops on the shoreline. Italy finally entered the war on 26 April 1915, giving Britain and France new bases in the Mediterranean, most importantly Naples, which was used to refuel and supply ships heading to and from Gallipoli and Salonika.

May Day saw the sinking of the American vessel *Gulflight*, the first US casualty sunk without warning. With 600 guns, the Germans attack toward Gorlice and Tarnow on 1 May too. Success is rapid and by the 6th both objectives are in German hands. On the 6th, in the Dardanelles, a second attempt to capture Krithia, close to Cape Helles, fails. 6,500 casualties saw a gain of 600 yards. Meanwhile, General Sir Horace Smith-Dorrien is relieved of command after suggesting a tactical withdrawal from the Ypres salient.

The U-20 sinks the Cunard liner *Lusitania* off Queenstown on 7 May 1915, with the loss of 124 Americans among its 1,198 dead. Winston Churchill uses the disaster to attempt to force America's hand to join the war but he is unceremoniously sacked on 26 May after the obvious failures in the Dardanelles. On the same day, the Italians introduce a naval blockade of Austro-Hungarian forces. HMS *Majestic* was lost to the submarine U-21 off Cape Helles on the 27th with the deaths of forty-nine of her crew. She was the third battleship of the Gallipoli campaign to be torpedoed in a fortnight.

News from the Western Front is bad with counter attacks failing on the Ypres salient. The Germans capture Frenzenberg Ridge on the 8th. With the British attacking Aubers Ridge, the French counter against Artois. On the 11th, British forces gather for the attack on Baghdad while in Africa, on the next day, Botha demands unconditional surrender after capturing Windhoek. Internment of all enemy aliens in Britain is ordered on the 13th. A huge shortage of artillery shells sees British attacks on Festubert in support of the French at Artois not being pressed home. By the 24th, the Battle of Ypres is fizzling out. A German attack has limited success and by the 25th, it is over. The casualty list is high: 58,000 British, 35,000 German and 10,000 French! Britain forms a coalition government, with Lloyd George becoming Minister of Munitions.

Britain's attack on Festubert ends on 27 May with a mile's worth of ground over a 3,000 yard front being won at the cost of 16,000 dead and seriously injured. The Germans lose 5,000. With poison gas being a major factor in the war, French bombers attack chemical plants at Ludwigshafen. It is the first major French long range bombing raid.

After the sinking of the *Gulflight*, the German government issues an apology to the USA on 1 June. Meanwhile, the fallout of the *Lusitania* sinking continued. Troopships hurried to the Dardanelles with more troops, while a fleet of hospital ships, including the world's largest four-funnelled liners, ferry the wounded back to Mudros and to hospitals all over the Mediterranean and also Britain. Finally, British seapower settles the *Königsberg* problem when British monitors, directed by spotter plane, shell the German cruiser for ninety minutes. Her German crew scuttle the *Königsberg* but her guns are salvaged.

On 3 June, advances by the Central Powers see Przemysl recaptured. An attempt by the British to attack the Turkish town of Krithia for the third time fails yet again. A few hundred yards are taken at the cost of 6,500 out of 30,000 troops. The air war steps up with Zeppelin attacks on the night of 6/7 June against London and Hull. L9 causes sixty-four casualties in a mere twenty minutes over Hull, while three Zeppelins attack London. LZ38 manages to return to Belgium but is destroyed at its base by naval aircraft. A British pilot chases the LZ34 from Ostend to Ghent and destroys it by dropping bombs on it from above. LZ39 makes it safely back to its base. Despite the loss of the two airships, the effects on Britain are huge. By the 18th, the Battle of Artois is almost over, with the attacks on Vimy Ridge failing. The French claim to have recaptured around 25 sq. km of territory. In the East, Austro-Hungarian forces reoccupy Lemberg on the 22nd. A day later, Italy opens up a new front when she attacks in north east Italy in the First Battle of the Isonzo. The river is a major obstacle, as are the mountains at its Austrian side and they prevent the incursion of the Italian troops into Austria.

In July, the E11 comes back from a successful tour of the Black Sea, having

Above: The greatest civilian tragedy of Britain's war was the sinking of the *Lusitania* in May 1915. 1,198 died as she succumbed to a German torpedo. Unarmed and with no escort in waters known to harbour an enemy submarine, she had been a sitting duck.

sunk many Turkish vessels. In three tours of the Dardanelles, she had sunk some eighty ships. An Italian attack along the Isonzo on 5 July sees some 4,000 Italian dead in the battle for Gorizia. Four days later, the remaining German troops in German South West Africa surrender. Lord Kitchener calls for greater recruitment and two million answer the call to arms, many being formed into 'Pals' battalions, formed from workplaces and towns all over the country. 120,000 German troops attack Warsaw on 13 July and enter the city by 5 August. British women march on the 17th and demand to make a contribution to the war effort. Bulgaria secretly signs an agreement with the Central Powers and, despite denials, receives huge amounts of land. Between 18 July and 3 August, the inconclusive Second Battle of the Isonzo is fought. In Mesopotamia, the British advance up the Euphrates and defeat the Turkish at Nasiriya on 24 July.

Max Immelmann scores his first victory on 1 August 1915 using a Fokker with interrupter device. It signals the start of a period of German dominance in the air war. Edith Cavell, a British nurse, is arrested in Belgium for helping some 200 prisoners of war to escape. Despite international condemnation, she is tried and executed in October.

Meanwhile, on 6 August a final attempt is made to break the deadlock in Turkey, with an invasion at Suvla Bay in an attempt to outflank the Turks. Marine artist and inventor of dazzle paint, Norman Wilkinson, is an RNR officer during the invasion. Despite the bravery of the troops on the ground, failures in leadership

WITH MALICE
TOWARDS NONE,
WITH CHARITY FOR
ALL WITH FIRMNESS
IN THE RIGHT, AS
GOD GIVES US TO
SEE THE RIGHT
- LINCOLN

VON BERNSTORFF
CHARGES
BREACH IN
SPIRIT OF
AMERICAN
NEUTRALITY

[From the " New York Sun," April 13, 1915.

THE AMERICAN NOTE.

From the *New York Sun*, April 1915. Despite the sinking of the *Lusitania* in May, President Woodrow Wilson would not allow the USA to be drawn into the war. Instead, the Americans and the Germans continued a war of words conducted through a series of official letters.

see the Turks again retain the high ground and the invasion is doomed. Despite requests for almost 100,000 reinforcements on 17 August, the political will at home is lacking.

On the 12th, engineers in Lincoln begin work on *Little Willie*, the first armoured tank. A week later, the White Star liner *Arabic* is sunk, with the loss of three Americans. Next day, the Italians declare war on Turkey. Czar Nicholas takes full command of the Russian forces on 21 August and Brest-Litovsk is captured from the Russians on 25 August. On the 26th, the Germans announce that no longer will liners be attacked without warning. General Sir Charles Townshend is ordered to advance against Kut-el-Amara on the Tigris. He declares his 11,000 troops are not enough but is sent against 10,000 entrenched Turkish troops on 12 September. The Russians receive offers of peace from Germany but on 28 August refuse to agree until all German troops have left Russian soil.

September sees the Bulgarians mobilise on the 22nd after meeting with the Central Powers on the 6th. By 18 September, the German U-boats were withdrawn from the Channel and the south-western approaches. Transported in sections by rail, many U-boats head for the Mediterranean and a new campaign. The opening of the campaign in Serbia leads to an increased traffic in troopships to Salonika in the Eastern Mediterranean to prevent the Central Powers and Bulgaria capturing the Balkan state. On 25 September, the Western Front sees the end of a three-day bombardment in the Champagne region by the French, who then attack. It is one of three simultaneous attacks designed to give some relief to the Russians in the East. Despite early gains, including a short holding of the Vimy Ridge, some 78,000 French and Germans are wounded or killed. The British attack in what becomes known as the Battle of Loos and, for the first time in the war, the British use gas. This comes about due to the shortage of artillery shells. Adverse winds blow the gas back onto the British lines. Some 4,000 yards are captured but the German second line holds.

On 27 September, the Greek government agrees to 150,000 French and British troops using Salonika as a base. In Mesopotamia, the British capture Kut-el-Amara. The Turks lose 4,000 dead and injured with 1,300 captured. British losses are 1,230. Despite successes in Mesopotamia, the British continue the pull out from the Dardanelles, with the 10th Division leaving there for Salonika.

Bulgarian troops attack Serbia on 14 October, with German and Austro-Hungarian armies attacking across the northern border. The Serbian army comes close to being surrounded but many escape and are forced to retreat to the south-west. The previous night, a concerted attack by Zeppelin raiders leaves 150 casualties in London. Britain declares war on Bulgaria on the 15th, and sees heavy casualties at the end of the Battle of Loos. 62,000 are lost for 26,000 Germans killed, wounded or captured. Between 18 October and 4 November, the Italians again attack over the Isonzo. Again, they make limited progress and the attacks are called off. By the 5th, the Serbian army is cut off from its allies and an unbroken railway line runs from Berlin to Turkey after the fall of the important railway junction of Nis. Again, the Italians attack over the Isonzo, failing to make any progress but effectively flattening the town of Gorizia with artillery fire. Another 49,000 Italians are dead or wounded for no gain.

Yet another enemy outrage sees the Austrian submarine U-38 shell and then sink the liner *Ancona* on 7 November, with the loss of 208 dead, including twenty-five Americans. Lord Kitchener visits Gallipoli on 22 November. He advocates evacuation and, by 7 December, the government agrees to withdraw from Suvla Bay and Ari Burna. The work of evacuation begins the following day. With no opposition from the Turks, 83,000 men, 186 guns, 4,500 mules and horses and 1,700 motor vehicles are salvaged from the disastrous campaign. On 7 December, numerically superior Turkish troops lay siege to Kut-el-Amara. On 12 December, a withdrawal by sea from Albania takes place. Field Marshal Sir John French is removed from leadership of the British Expeditionary Force on 17 December and is replaced by General Sir Douglas Haig. A German commerce raider, the *Moewe*, left Bremen on Boxing Day 1915, sinking fourteen ships between then and March. The end of the year saw the evacuation from Cape Helles begin, marking the end of the Gallipoli campaign. There would be no victories to celebrate for New Year 1916 and the war had somehow managed to drag on for another year. Conscription was introduced in the dying days of the year of 1915. The War to end all Wars was not yet over. Its deadliest days were to come! 29 December saw General Joffre of France and General Haig meet. They will discuss 1916 and an attack that will be planned along the Somme river in spring 1916. Kitchener's Pals Battalions will have finished their military training by then and it will be time to throw them into the fray. Despite the huge casualty rate on all fronts, 1915 will be looked back on as preparation for the bloodbath that will ensue in the coming year.

Left: 'The Year of Victory.' A German soldier passing the Pillar of Victory in Berlin and saying that he must march further before receiving his wreath. Published in *Lustige Blatter* on the first anniversary of the start of the First World War.

JANUARY 1915

A pair of Tommies rummage through a pile of boots worn through by heavy marching. Keeping the soldiers supplied with such essentials would become as big a logistical challenge as the need for shells.

Life in the trenches

By 1915 the opposing forces fighting on the Western Front had become so firmly entrenched that their governments looked to the east for a possible breakthrough in the war. Meanwhile, trench life settled into a routine, the methods of creating the trenches and defences, including barbed wire entanglements, firmly established. These views are of the German side.

Above: A German field gun in action. At this stage in the war the gunners are still wearing their Pickelhaube, the spiked helmets, albeit with cloth covers to make them less conspicuous. They wouldn't start to replace them until early 1916, when the coal-scuttle Stalhelm was introduced.

Below: Camouflaged shelters behind the German lines.

The First World War saw several significant technological advances, not least of which was the field telephone. These photographs show the German equipment in use. Obviously the telephones provided instantaneous communication, but as with the telegraph system, they did require miles of wires which had to be strung across the countryside. Dispatch riders and messengers would still play their part in conveying messages and information, especially on the battlefield.

When the fighting stops a semblance of normal life goes on. *Above:* Pay day on the battlefield for these German soldiers, and, below, buying grapes from a fruit stall in a Belgian town.

Above: French soldiers construct a reserve trench behind the firing lines.

Below: The Kaiser and General von Emmich at the German headquarters in France.

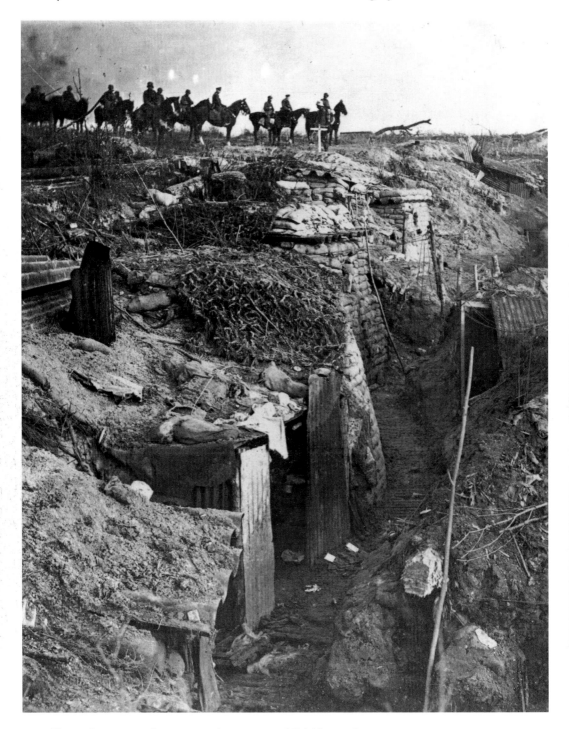

Above: German cavalrymen examine a captured British trench.

Above: During the winter of 1914–15, a British patrol pauses to pay a silent tribute to the graves of the fallen from the Loyal North Lancashire Regiment.

Zeppelin raid on the east coast

On the night of 19/20 January 1915 Germany launches its first Zeppelin raids when the L3 and
L4 cross the Norfolk coast after their plan to attack the Humber was foiled by bad weather.
Instead, they drop their bombs on Great Yarmouth, above, and King's Lynn, shown below.

In the early stages of the war the Zeppelin crews travelled in open gondolas, shown top, and these were only enclosed as the war progressed. On the one hand the Zeppelins became bigger and better equipped, but they also had to fly ever higher to evade the improved defensive measures, both in the form of better anti-aircraft guns and also new fighter aircraft.

Above: Lady to policeman. 'Oh, have you seen the Zeppelin? Which way did it go?' Policeman (in best official manner). 'Up the street opposite, madam, and first turning on the left.' *Punch* cartoon, November 1915.

Below: With anxiety etched on their faces, a group of Parisians pause in the street to watch as a German aircraft flies over the city.

Above: HMS *Tiger* and *Renown* on patrol in the North Sea. *Tiger* was the most heavily armoured of the battlecruisers launched prior to the war and served at the Battle of Dogger Bank in early 1915 and at Jutland, where despite several hits, she was relatively unscathed. She had cost some £2.53 million to build at John Brown's Clydebank shipyard. *Renown* was not commissioned until September 1916.

The Battle of Dogger Bank

Admiral David Beatty, shown right, led the First Battlecruiser Squadron at the battles of Heligoland Bight in 1914, Dogger Bank in 1915 and at Jutland in 1916. Beatty himself was born in Cheshire in 1871 and his first command was HMS *Arrogant* in 1903. By 1910, he was a rear admiral and in 1914 was promoted to vice-admiral. He kept command of the First Battlecruiser Squadron for the early part of the war until he was promoted to commander-in-chief of the Grand Fleet.

Above: Blücher was the last German armoured cruiser. Designed to match the Invincible class of cruisers, she was larger than previous German vessels and carried twelve 21-cm guns in expectation of the British ships having 9-in guns. In reality, *Invincible* was fitted with 12-in guns, but it was too late to adjust the design of *Blücher*. At the Battle of Dogger Bank on 23 January 1915, *Blücher* was hit numerous times by the British battlecruisers and HMS *Aurora* sent a salvo of torpedoes into her side that saw *Blücher* sink. The ship capsized, her crew on her side as she went down. Over 900 died. More may have been saved but a Zeppelin crew overhead thought she was British and scared away the destroyers rushing to save the crew.

Above: Admiral Beatty and his officers.

Below: SMS *Seydlitz*, along with *Blücher, Moltke, Von der Tann* and *Derfflinger* and numerous light cruisers and destroyers, had shelled the English East Coast towns in December and would meet the British fleet at Dogger Bank in January. *Seydlitz* herself was damaged by HMS *Lion* at Dogger Bank, when a 13.5-in shell destroyed a rear turret.

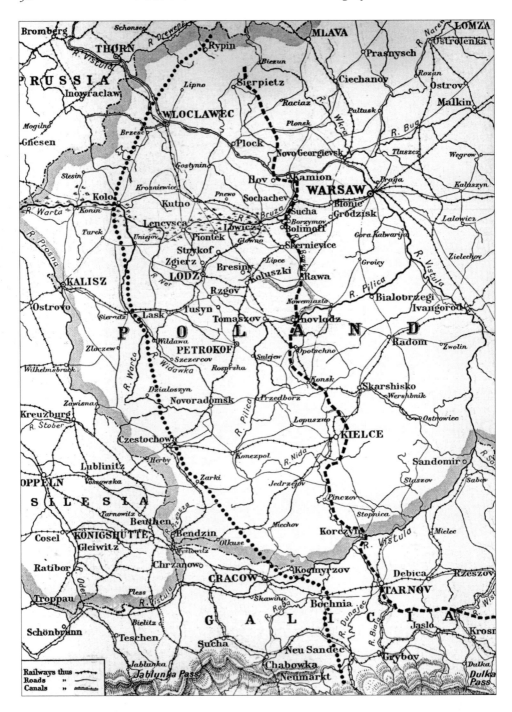

The Eastern Front

Map of the main eastern theatre of war at the start of 1915, showing Warsaw and the Galicia region to the south. In the latter part of 1914 the Russian forces had pushed back the German Ninth Army, resulting in heavy losses. The situation remained fluid over the ensuing months.

It had been a dramatic turn of fortunes for the Germans. In October 1914 Hindenburg's divisions had reached almost into Warsaw itself, but facing stiff opposition from the Russians were forced to withdraw. *Above:* German troops rest during their retreat. *Below:* Damage caused to an unidentified town in East Prussia by the advancing Russian artillery.

Above: A German machine gun section holds a barricade in Poland. In November Hindenburg had sought to surround the Russians at Lodz, but the offensive was rebuffed, but at least he had halted the Russian advance towards Prussia.

Above: German prisoners being marched through the streets of Warsaw. *Below:* An open air banquet given by the Russian officers to celebrate their victory over the 'German invaders'. But Hindenburg was already planning a new push towards the capital in late January 1915, and this time he would use a deadly new weapon, poison gas.

Japan's involvement

Shortly before the outbreak of the First World War the Japanese government had affirmed that it would do its part to aid the British, as laid down in the Anglo-Japanese Alliance. Consequently on 15 August 1914 an ultimatum was issued to the Germans demanding their withdrawal from the region. One of the first tasks had been to capture the German base at Tsingtao, China, accomplished in November 1914.

Left: Lieutenant-General Kamio, who had been in charge of the Tsingtao force, with General Barnardiston.

Below: One of the Japanese seige guns that had brought about the fall of Tsingtao. Note the field telephone.

Above: Japanese gun in action against the German stronghold. The black smoke is rising from one of the oil tanks which had been set on fire. These soldiers relax after the fall of Tsingtao.

Battle of Bolimov

31 January: The Germans initiated an advance towards Warsaw, in what became known as the Battle of Bolimov, by bombarding the Russians with 18,000 poison gas shells, its first use in the war. Fortunately the cold conditions and the wind minimised the effects of the gas, although many Russian soldiers were treated at a Red Cross station, shown above.

FEBRUARY 1915

A British gun team trudges through the mud hauling a '47' field gun on the Western Front. The 4.7-inch guns had provided excellent service in the Boer War and were now used to plug the gaps until the batteries could be requipped with the bigger BL 60-pdr.

Submarine warfare

1915 saw the start of unrestricted submarine warfare. Before this, crews had a chance to abandon ship before the submarine's gun was used to sink their vessel, or charges laid. Torpedoes were expensive and submarines had limited quantities. *Above:* This crew have been allowed to abandon ship before their ship has been destroyed.

Above: The submarine U-20 which had begun the reign of unrestricted submarine warfare at the start of 1915. It was her that sank the *Lusitania* too. In November 1916, she grounded off Denmark and was destroyed. The conning tower of U-20 is on display in a Danish museum.

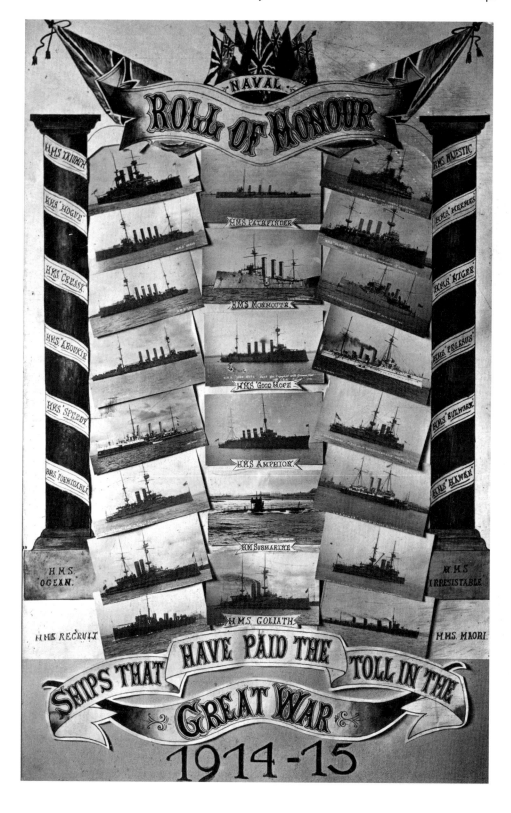

Above: A German submarine leaves on patrol. At this stage of the war, many submarines still operated in shallow waters around the coasts. The ports of Ostend and Zeebrugge gave the Germans access to many areas previously unavailable due to the range of the submarines.

Below: The U-36 used its tender, the fishing boat W-2, as a screen to capture the Dutch ferry *Batavier V* in March 1915. Despite being neutral, Dutch steamers still sailed to the UK and the Germans wanted to prevent war materiel being transported to or from Holland.

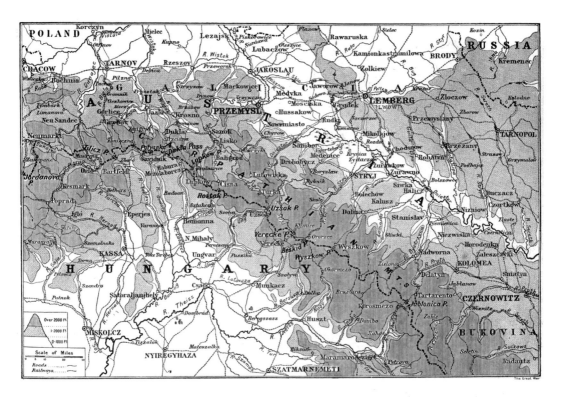

The Battle of Bolimov

Above: Map of the Przemysl region. The Battle of Bolimov was a diversionary tactic, with the German and Austro-Hungarian forces poised to strike into Russia from East Prussia in the north, and also through the province of Galicia, which was in Russian hands.

During February the Russian line was pushed back 70 miles with around 90,000 of the Russians troops taken prisoner.

Right: A German Lancer scout.

Above: General von Gropp, with his Chief of Staff, examines a trench recently abandoned by the retreating Russians forces in Poland.

Left: A Russian trench that is still occupied. The soldiers have their bayonets fixed at the ready for a charge.

Above: German artillerymen greet their Austrian allies beside a roadside shrine in the snow-covered Carpathians.

Below: Austrian gunners prepare to fire their heavy howitzers.

During the push into Poland a troop of Germany's Death's Head Hussars rest after a march, shown above, and a gun team in the Carpathians is shown below.

Above: Barges are utilised to take the German troops and their supplies across the River Niemen and towards Russian territory.

The German and Austro-Hungarian advance through Galicia continued throughout February 1915. German transport crossing a river in the Galicia region, shown above.

Below: An Austrian trench in newly occupied Russian territory.

A 28-ton Austrian siege howitzer, top, and a German field gun. Both are seen in Galicia.

Above: German artillery units passing through a town in the Galicia region.

Below: A German Red Cross contingent on the move in Poland.

The Middle East

Above: An Ottoman camel corps at Beersheba. Substantial Ottoman forces had crossed the Sinai Peninsula, but their attack on the Suez Canal in early January failed when they encountered strong defences held by the British. A second assault on 3 February resulted in heavy losses. Arabian troops, mobilised and equipped by the Turks, are shown below.

Many German and Turkish prisoners from the Dardanelles were taken to Cairo, which served as the main base for Britain's forces in the region. *Above:* Wounded Turkish prisoners are accompanied by nurses in the grounds of the new Red Cross hospital. *Below:* The first batch of German and Turkish prisoners are marched through Cairo under Australian escort.

New Zealand troops in Egypt. On fatigue duty, above, and, below, during a bridge building exercise near the Nile, in preparation for the forthcoming Dardanelles landings.

Changes to the soldiers' clothing and equipment came only gradually for some of the combatants. The French in particular were notoriously slow in adapting their gear to the new conditions in the field. At the start of the war, and until 1915, they were still wearing the unifrom of the Franco-Prussian war era, with blue tunics and red trousers. Here they are shown wearing a new type of protective headgear, a steel helmet that is worn over the top of their cloth caps. The M15 Adrian helmet with its peak and distinctive top ridge, would become the standard headgear for the French Army.

MARCH 1915

On 18 March 1915, HMS *Irresistible* hit a mine off the Turkish coast. With her crew rescued, she slowly drifted into the range of Turkish guns and was sunk. This view was photographed from HMS *Lord Nelson*, which took off many of the crew.

South Africa

On 18 March 1915, General Louis Botha led 21,000 troops in the main invasion of German South-west Africa. *Above:* South African troopers attend a church service at Pretoria before joing in the pursuit of the rebels. *Below:* A British force enters German territory at a point near Raman's Drift. The capital, Windhoek, is occupied on 12 May and Botha calls upon the Germans for an unconditional surrender.

Above: The Canadian Northern Line's *Royal George* at Port Said on 28 March 1915, with marines of the Royal Naval Division aboard. The marines were heading for the Dardanelles. The *George's* sister *Royal Edward* was sunk on 13 August 1915 when she was torpedoed by the UB-14 with the loss of around 1,000 men.

The Dardanelles Campaigns

The initial plans in the Dardanelles were to force Turkey into submission using the might of the combined navies of Britain and France, with assistance from Russian and Australian forces. The narrow strait between European and Asian Turkey was a major pinch point between the Mediterranean and Black Sea. Attempts by submarines to enter the heavily protected strait proved dangerous and often fatal. Ottoman guns protected the entrance as well as the route. In late 1914, the British and French planned a naval blockade and bombardment of the strait, as well as disruption of Ottoman shipping in the Sea of Marmara.

At the start of the war, Turkey was not aligned with either the Central Powers or the Allies but were siding with the Germans, who had given them two warships. After diplomatic wrangling and the confiscation of two warships building in British yards, the Turks declared the Dardanelles closed to Allied shipping in early October 1914. On the 28th, they bombarded Russian ships in an attempt to destroy their Black Sea Fleet and the bases they operated from. On 2 November, Russia declared war on the Ottoman Empire and called for assistance from France and Britain in January 1915. Plans were already in motion to capture the Dardanelles and Winston Churchill, First Sea Lord, presented a plan to the Prime Minister, Asquith, for approval. The attack on the Dardanelles would give a supply route to the Russians that could easily be operated all year round, with ease of access to the Eastern Front too. The Baltic route had been cut off and journeys to Siberia and the far north of Russia could only easily be undertaken from spring until autumn. With a lack of troops available, the naval attack on Turkey was given the go-ahead.

On 3 November 1914, the first British attack was made, even before Britain had declared war on Turkey, by HMS *Indomitable* and *Indefatigable*, with the French *Suffren* and *Verite* in support. Designed to test the defences, this was a prelude to the naval bombardment that would begin at 7.30 a.m. on 19 February 1915. The first shot was fired by the Turks as two destroyers probed the straits. HMS *Cornwallis* and *Vengeance* engaged the forts but the shelling was ineffectual. On 25 February another attempt was made. With the Turks abandoning the outer ring of forts, Royal Marines landed to set explosive charges. The minefields across the straits prevented incursions but little effort was made to clear them. The mineweeper crews in their converted trawlers were unwilling to be under fire from both sides of the straits. On 13 March, HMS *Amethyst* and six trawlers attempted to clear the mines but four of the trawlers and *Amethyst* were hit.

18 March saw a battle ensue. A new line of mines had been laid on the 8th and the plan was to silence the defences for the first five minefields and destroy them. Fourteen British ships and four outdated French pre-Dreadnoughts took part. The Allies were unaware of the new set of mines and lack of intelligence from minesweepers that had discovered the new mines meant that the fleet sailed

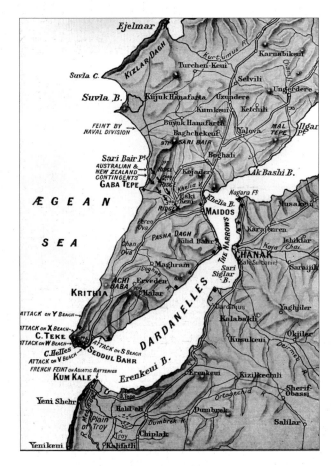

Map of the Dardanelles and the Gallipoli Peninsula, showing the location of the operations in the spring of 1915.

Above: Colonial and Senegalese troops ready to embark for the Dardanelles at Mudros, a port on the Greeks' Mediterranean island of Lemnos. The harbour at Lemnos was broad enough to accept the British and French warships and it was placed under the control of the British for operations against the Dardanelles. *Below:* British forces embarking at Lemnos.

Above: Lancashire Fusiliers ready to land at Gallipoli.

The Dardanelles landings were completed using rowing boats launched from the sides of both merchant and naval vessels. The element of surprise was difficult to achieve. *Below:* Australians landing on the exposed beach.

into them. At 1.54 p.m. the French *Bouvet* hit a mine and capsized with the loss of 639 crew. *Inflexible* then hit a mine, killing thirty crew, but was successfully beached. Next to succumb was *Irresistible*. Attempts by HMS *Ocean* to take her in tow only caused the mining of this ship too. Her steering gear was broken and she drifted helplessly. The Turks, for the loss of 118 dead, had caused the sinking of three battleships, with the damage of another. Some 700 had died too on the Allied side, most on *Bouvet*. The one saving grace was that the ships used were old and expendable, even if their crews were not easily replaceable. By 23 March, it was obvious that sea warfare would not decide the Dardanelles campaign and that land forces would be required. An invasion was planned.

In the meantime, many attempts had been made to get through the straits by submarine. The first sub to get past the minefields was the B11, which sank the *Mesudiye* near Canakkale on 13 December. She had successfully passed five of the ten minefields. Her commander, Lt-Cmdr Norman Holbrook, was awarded the first naval VC of the war. On 15 January, a French submarine, *Saphir*, passed the narrows but ran aground at Nagara Point. On 17 April, the British tried again, with E15 running aground and being shelled. Seven of her crew were killed and the rest captured. HMAS AE2 succeeded in getting through the straits on the night of 24/25 April and sank an Ottoman cruiser but was spotted and rammed. Next through was HMS E14, which spent three weeks in a campaign that struck fear into the Turks. Three times E14 made the journey, for which her captain won the VC. The next VC winner was Martin Nasmith, whose E11 sank or disabled eleven ships in May. Men landed from submarines operated a guerilla war, blowing up

Below: HMS *Queen Elizabeth* in the Dardanelles, March 1915. The naval efforts to take the Dardanelles had failed and the loss of ships saw the Navy withdraw its new Dreadnought in May 1915.

Above: HMS *Queen Elizabeth* was just too valuable to lose to a Turkish mine. She would survive both wars and was eventually broken up in Dalmuir, Scotland, in 1948.

bridges and strategic targets along the coast. French submarines also made the dangerous journey but were less successful. For the loss of eight submarines, the Allies had sunk one battleship, one destroyer, five gunboats, as well as eleven troop transports, forty-four supply vessels and 148 sailing ships.

With the failure of the seaborne attacks, it was obvious that a landing would have to be made on the Dardanelles. The idea was that the British would land at Cape Helles and that Australian and New Zealand Army Corps (or ANZAC) troops would land at Gaba Tepe. It was to be the largest amphibious attack of the war. The British landed in the right place on 25 April 1915 but the ANZAC troops landed too far north. With support from the navy, the troops landed successfully. At V beach, the cargo steamer *River Clyde* was used to land some 2,000 men. Men went ashore in the boats of the battleships, which gave covering fire. At Cape Helles, five beaches were used and the troops landed after a naval bombardment. At ANZAC Cove, the attacks were a surprise with no bombardment beforehand.

It was soon obvious, as British and ANZAC troops failed to take their objectives, or even get close to them, that the landings were not a success. The Turks had put up a spirited defence, much stronger than expected. In May, naval support was severely diminished after the sinking of HMS *Goliath* on 12 May, *Triumph* off

Anzac Cove on 25 May and *Majestic*, sunk off W Beach on 27 May. Permanent naval support was simply withdrawn with the brand new HMS *Queen Elizabeth* being sent back to the UK.

The campaign was a huge failure. The Turks knew of the forthcoming invasion and had prepared for it. Not only were the guns in the forts defending the straits mobile but they had defended the likely landing points. Delays in the expected landing saw much preparation work that would leave the Allies in a dangerous position. Those landing from the *River Clyde* were mauled by the machine guns, which peppered the men as they tried to land. Of the first 200 to leave the ship, a mere twenty-one reached the shore. Turkey's 57th Regiment fought to the last, with every member either dead or seriously wounded in the attacks. Sixty and seventy per cent casualty rates were the norm for those landing on some beaches, including 600 of 1,000 of the Lancashire Regiment. Six Victoria Crosses were awarded to the men of the regiment for the action during the landings. Of 1,012 Dublin and Munster Fusiliers, only eleven survived the Gallipoli Campaign unscathed.

Most men stayed close to the beaches and the Turks had time to reinforce their troops. A small number of Royal Naval Air Service aircraft provided air support, as did seaplanes from the seaplane tenders such as HMS *Ben-my-Chree* and HMS *Ark Royal*. The aircraft gave aerial reconnaissance and were used for artillery spotting.

On 27 April, the Turks attacked, intent on sending the invaders back to the beaches again at Anzac Cove. The Turks were held at bay and on the next day, British troops attacked towards Krithia. With 3,000 dead or wounded, the attack stalled half way to Krithia. With more Turkish reinforcements joining the fray, the opportunity for a quick victory had gone. On 30 April reinforcements in the shape of the Royal Naval Division arrived. The Turks attacked the same day but were repulsed by heavy machine gun fire. In May, many of the troops from Anzac Cove go to Cape Helles and reinforcements came from Egypt. On 6 May, after a heavy bombardment, some 20,000 troops moved to attack, with the objectives of capturing Krithia, Kereves Dere and Achi Baba. Heavy artillery fire from hidden Turkish guns stopped the attacks. The next day, reinforcements arrived but they could make little progress and dug in close to their objectives. The Allies were running low on supplies and new stocks of ammunition had to be delivered before more attacks were possible.

The Turks counter-attacked on 19 May against the 17,000 ANZAC troops at Anzac Cove with some 42,000 troops. With few artillery pieces, they hoped to overpower the Allied troops by strength alone. Unfortunately, their preparations had been spotted and the ANZAC troops forewarned. 10,000 Turkish troops were wounded and 3,000 killed for the loss of 168 killed and 468 injured on the Allied side. Like the British, the Turks lacked sufficient artillery ammunition and this, and the losses at Anzac, saw the stopping of frontal assaults.

June saw another attack on Krithia on the 4th but this failed once more. Like their Western Front counterparts, the troops had dug in for the duration. June and July would see attack and counter attack, with little being gained by either side

The Anniversary Bouquet
Bernhardi: 'Have I not surpassed your most sanguine expectations?' Dutch artist Louis Raemaekers' take on the first anniversary of the Great War in August 1915.

Above: 1915, The Second Battle of Ypres, by Richard Jack. *(Canadian War Museums Library & Archives)*

Left: The Second Battle of Ypres saw the use of poisonous chlorine gas by the Germans. 'Fancy, how nice! They are drinking death in their sleep.' Another dawing by Raemaekers, showing the gas being released from cylinders. As the war progressed gas was used by both sides and usually delivered by special shells.

Opposite: By 1915, the Western Front had descended into a slogging match and the Eastern Front and the Middle East appeared to offer opportunites for more significant gains. This map of the area was published in *The Times History of the War* in 1915. It shows the position of the Russian Front in August 1915, and again in October that year. Note the considerable German Austro-Hungarian gains.

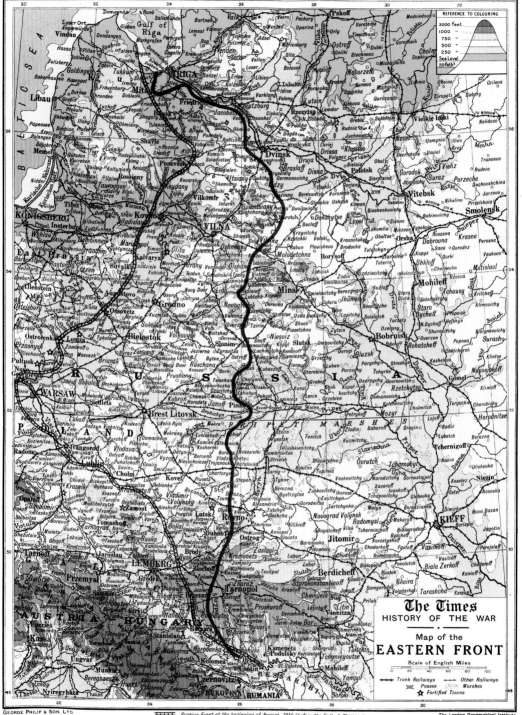

The Times
HISTORY OF THE WAR

Map of the
EASTERN FRONT

Scale of English Miles

Trunk Railways   Other Railways
Passes   Marshes
Fortified Towns

GEORGE PHILIP & SON, LTD.

Russian Front at the beginning of August, 1915 (before the Fall of Warsaw).
Russian Front towards the end of October, 1915.

The London Geographical Institute

REFERENCE TO COLOURING
2000 feet
1000
750
500
250
Sea Level
20 fath.

H.M.S. FORMIDABLE PASSING THE KING. JULY 20TH 1914

Rule, Britannia, Britannia rule the waves;

Left: Three typical wartime postcards. All three are jingoistic in their nature, with the first commemorating a royal visit to the Fleet immediately prior to the declaration of war. Admiral Jellicoe is shown in the middle view while the bottom postcard proclaims Britain's dominance at sea.

Above: HMS *Triumph* was the second of two Swiftsure class battleships. It was launched in 1903 and sunk off Gaba Tepe by a German torpedo, launched from U-21, during the Dardanelles landings in May 1915.

Right: The Entente Cordiale of 1904 was a major agreement between the French and the British, basically paving the way for a war with Britain and France against Germany. The agreement helped to resolve disputes over parts of Britain's and France's empires and made the threat of war between the two nations a thing of the past. They would agree to closer co-operation in some foreign affairs while subtly ignoring each other's claims over parts of the other's foreign acquisitions.

BRITISH AND FRENCH SAILORS.
ENTENTE CORDIALE

The Dardanelles Campaign
Norman Wilkinson, the famous marine artist, was at Gallipoli during the landings there. The top view shows HMS *Exmouth* at Kephalo, straddled by two cargo vessels. The lower one is of a Welsh casualty dressing station on A Beach, Gallipoli.

Above: The French flagship *Suffren* flying the flag off the French Contre Amiral Geupratte.

Below: Shells falling on the base camp at Cape Helles during the landings.

IRISHMEN AVENGE THE LUSITANIA

JOIN AN IRISH REGIMENT

ISSUED BY THE CENTRAL COUNCIL FOR THE ORGANISATION OF RECRUITING IN IRELAND.   John Shuley & Co. Dublin.   W. P. 110—7,800. 5'15

Above: The tragic sight of the mighty Cunarder *Lusitania* making its way to the bottom of the sea, around 350 feet below, was used as a propaganda image to encourage more men to volunteer for the army, especially the Irish, who had not joined up in the same way as those in the rest of Britain had.

Below: Aquitania was just one of many huge hospital ships required during the Dardanelles campaign. The smaller hospital ship is transshipping the seriously injured for repatriation to Blighty!

Left: German poster by Max Mandl. 'Now for a short time only, an exhibition of spoils from the air war campaign.' Note the broken British biplane.

Opposite: Warneford's destruction of the LZ 38, in June 1915, brought a much needed victory against the Zeppelin raiders. Flying a Morane monoplane he had dropped bombs on the top of the airship. Later progress with aircraft capabilities and incendiary bullets, to ignite the hydrogen gas, would turn the tables on the aerial leviathans.

Below: The seaplane base at Kephalo. The aircraft performed vital duties, acting as artillery spotters.

WOHLFAHRT 15

Einweihung
am 21. Oktober
am Paradeplatz
Nagelkarten im Vorverkauf
an den mit Plakaten gekenn-
zeichneten Stellen.

Der eiserne Wehrmann

Königsberg 1915

Die Nagelung ist zum Besten der hinterbliebenen gefallener
Krieger des Ersten Armeekorps (Ostpreuß.) bestimmt.

H. M. DÖRRIN SOHN BERLIN C.2

Opposite: A German poster announcing the dedication of an Eiserne Wehrmann (Iron Warrior) to benefit the survivors of fallen soldiers of the First Army Corps in East Prussia. The artist is E. Wohlfahrt.

L'ENTENTE CORDIALE ♥
1915

JOURNÉE DU P[O...]

25 ET 26 DÉCEMBRE 1915
ORGANISÉE PAR LE PARLEMENT

Propaganda in the form of posters, prints and newspaper and magazine illustrations took many angles, either demonising the enemy, as shown above with the spider of Britain spinning its web across Europe, or romanticising the troops, as shown in this French example on the left. Note that the soldier is fighting in a cloth hat. Steel helmets would not become general issue for the main combatants until 1916 onwards.

"BE HONEST WITH YOURSELF. BE CERTAIN THAT YOUR SO-CALLED REASON IS NOT A SELFISH EXCUSE"

LORD KITCHENER

ENLIST TO-DAY

PUBLISHED BY THE PARLIAMENTARY RECRUITING COMMITTEE, LONDON. POSTER No 127.

PRINTED BY BEMROSE & SONS LTD LONDON & DERBY. W 8768/576

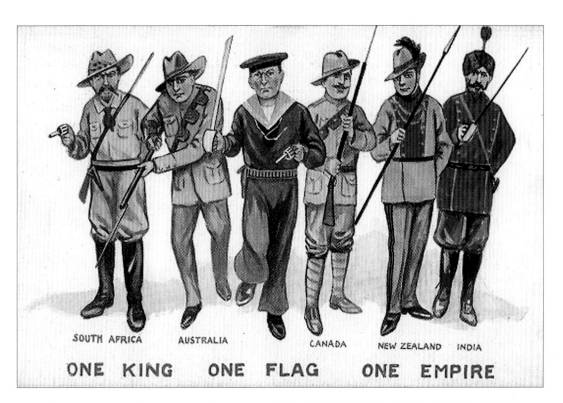

ONE KING   ONE FLAG   ONE EMPIRE

This page: Postcards were a popular and informal way of promulgating the message. The examples on this page are typical of the millions of cards produced during the war, with a rousing if somewhat crude depiction of the soldiers of the Empire, above, and the common theme of the end of a Zeppelin, right.

Opposite: Unlike the other combatants Britain relied on volunteers to fill the ranks in the first two years of the war. In an age before television, and with a high degree of illiteracy in the lower classes, the poster became a key and eye-catching element in the drive for new recruits. Designs were produced by individual printers and although approved by the Parliamentary Recruiting Commitee there was no overall coordination. The result was a mishmash of design styles, with a few excellent posters amid a sea of mediocrity. The quotation is from Lord Kitchener, but the psychological approach seems very tame by modern standards.

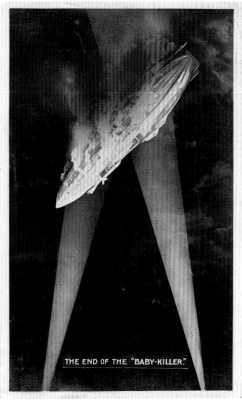

THE END OF THE "BABY-KILLER."

Until conscription was introduced in 1916, the recruiting posters took the form of appeals to the individual, and various schemes, such as the Pals Battalions, were devised to encourage more men to enlist.

The Anglo-French invasion of the Gallipoli Peninsula begins on 25 April 1915. The Australians are shown landing at Gaba Tepe. There are a number of pathways, but the hillside is covered by low bushes, providing cover for enemy guns and snipers.

apart from more new graveyards housing the dead. Fifteen Allied divisions now stood against sixteen Ottoman divisions.

6 August saw the invasion of Suvla Bay in an attempt to break the deadlock. With the Turks occupying the hills around, it was nigh on impossible for the British to progress beyond the beach. Despite numerous attacks and counter attacks, the landing was a failure. Thousands of troops died, with high casualty rates the norm. On 12 August the Sandringham Company of the Royal Norfolk Regiment

Above: Men of the Australian 10th Light Infantry in their trenches on the Gallipoli Peninsula.

Above: A pause in the fighting for the men of the Australian Light Horse.

disappeared into the fog, killed or captured by the Turks. On 21 August the last offensive battles took place. Within the month, troops were needed elsewhere and were beginning to be taken off the Turkish coast for action in Salonika.

With Bulgaria entering the war, and a supply chain possible from Germany to Constantinople, the tide had turned for the Allies at Gallipoli. Terrible weather in November and a precarious supply line were proving to be too much. Evacuation begins in December at Suvla and Anzac, with all troops safely off by 20 December. Unfortunately, large quantities of stores and ammunition fell into Turkish hands. By 28 December the decision had been made to evacuate Cape Helles and planning began for the withdrawal of troops. This would continue into January.

The evacuations proved to be the best organized parts of the campaign with little loss of life and despite estimates of up to 30,000 casualties, very few actually died in the evacuation. Much material was left behind, but some 508 mules and hundreds of horses that could not be evacuated were killed. Some 1,600 trucks were destroyed too. It was the end of a failure that had cost numerous battleships, tens of thousands of men and an unknown quantity of ammunition and supplies, all expended for nothing.

Turkish artillery, during preparations, above, and in action in Gallipoli, below. The low bushes provided excellent cover.

Above: A camp for Turkish forces fighting on the Gallipoli Peninsula. *Below:* A Turkish infantry column takes a brief rest.

During the 24 April landing at Gallipoli, the merchant ship *River Clyde* was run ashore with 2,000 troops aboard. The ship was in plain sight of the Turkish defenders and the gunfire so severe that many soldiers died as the ship was raked with shells and bullets. Waiting till nightfall before the disembarkation, six Victoria Crosses were won by members of the crew. *River Clyde* remained in situ for some time, providing shelter for soldiers and serving as a pier for more disembarkations.

On the Eastern Front
The Austrian garrison at Hurko Fort in Przemysl, Galicia, surrenders to the Russian forces on
22 March, but the defences have been left in ruins by the Austrians.

APRIL 1915

Above: A deadly fashion parade. In the spring of 1915 the use of gas brought a new horror and a new look to the Western Front and new respirators were developed to deal with the threat. It was used initially by the Germans against the Russians, then Britain and France followed suit. Different types of gas were used ranging from xylyl bromide, a tear gas, to more lethal types such as chlorine, phosgene and mustard gas. The latter wasespecially nasty as it burned the skin and could cause permanent blindness.

Opposite: A graphic portrayal of a gas attack on a poster.

Gas!

Above: Canadian troops reel as a greenish-yellow cloud of chlorine gas engulfs their trench during the Second Battle of Ypres. A hankerchief soaked in water, or in urine, provided only minimal protection. The heavy gas tended to settle and pool withinin the lower ground of the trenches. When the gas was unleashed for the first time, at sunrise on 22 April 1915, the Allied troops, mostly French and Algerian territorials, had fled in panic and the Germans were astounded by its effectiveness. Some 10,000 men were affected, and it is estimated that around half of them died of asphyxiation.

Opposite page: A selection of gas mask types ranging from Allied respirators, top, French masks for both man and his dog, and an early German respirator and gauze mask worn by a German medic.

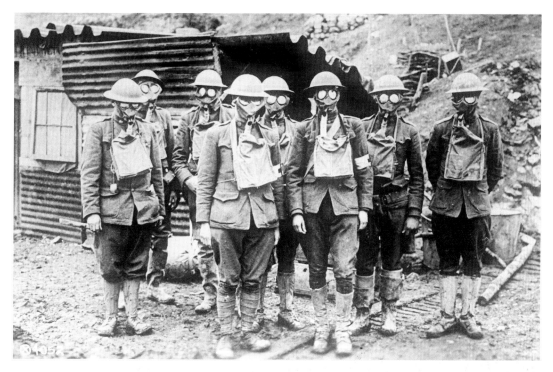

The Second Battle of Ypres

Left: Map showing the location of the Second Battle of Ypres, which began in April 1915. This was the only major attack by German forces on the Western Front that year, and was primarily intended to divert attention from the campaign against the Russians on the Eastern Front.

Below: A dramatic representation of the charge of the 4th Canadian Battalion at Ypres. Losses at the Second Battle of Ypres are estimated at around 69,000 for the Allies, and 35,000 for the Germans, with the huge difference resulting from the use of gas. Both sides would use it during the remainder of the war.

Above: A Canadian night attack through the woods at Ypres. The Canadian Scottish and 10th Battalion Canadian Infantry recapture the 4.7 guns.

Right: Punch's tribute to the Canadians who fought at Ypres. The simple caption states, 'CANADA! Ypres: April 22-24, 1915.'

The Armenian crisis

One of the greatest tragedies of the First World War was the treatment meted out to the Armenians by the Turks. Over one million died in the pogrom that began in 1915. These views show Armenian refugees escaping by boat and train from Turkish areas.

Naval aviation

This was in its infancy in 1915. Britain had realized the importance of seaplanes in 1914 and had various cross-channel steamers converted into seaplane carriers. *Above:* The Germans followed suit and this view shows a minelayer and seaplane in 1915. *Below:* A Sopwith fighter on a lighter. Attempts were made to fly land planes from naval vessels, as it was found that seaplanes could be easily damaged when being recovered or placed into the water.

From towing a lighter into the wind to making a temporary runway on top of a turret, it was a short step to designing ships with longer runways aboard. This view shows a biplane taking off from the second turret of HMS *Barham*. This ship was built by John Brown in Clydebank and was commissioned in 1915.

Above: HMS *Ark Royal* was the world's first ship designed from the outset to carry aircraft. She entered service on 10 December 1914 and was sent to the Mediterranean early in 1915 and was involved in the naval attacks in the Dardanelles in February. She could carry five floatplanes and four regular aircraft.

Below: Sailors from HMS *Hibernia* asleep on deck in 1915. Unlike soldiers at the Front, the sailors in the navy had long periods of rest. *Hibernia* holds the honour of being the first ship to launch an aircraft, when a biplane took off from her foredeck in May 1912. In 1915 she supported the Dardanelles campaign and was also used in the evacuation of troops from the area later in the year.

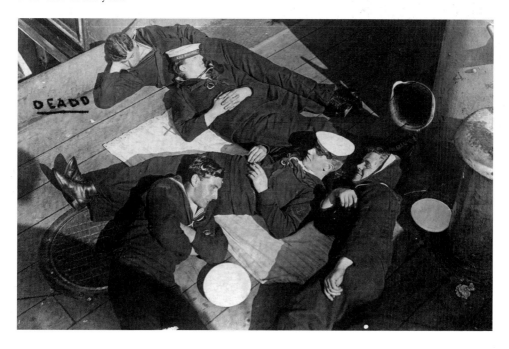

MAY 1915

The last plunge.

Lusitania sunk by a U-boat

Above: A propaganda postcard, one of a set of six, issued in Britain by the middle of May 1915. The sinking of the *Lusitania* saw the production of many posters, in memorium cards and even medals commemorating the loss of the Cunard superliner.

Opposite: 'Take Up the Sword of Justice' became the slogan following the sinking of the *Luisitania*. The stricken ship and many of its unfortunate passengers are depicted in the background on this poster.

Above: Lusitania at the Landing Stage, Liverpool. Even in wartime her route had not changed from her pre-war heyday. She still sailed from New York to Liverpool via Queenstown. She is shown below at the Cunard pier, New York.

Above: A funeral for victims of the *Lusitania.*
1,198 people were killed when the ship went down,
or drowned in the chilly Atlantic off the Old Head of
Kinsale. Some, like the young man on the right, were
lucky to be rescued by numerous fishing boats from
the small harbours on the Cork coast.

U-20

January 1915 saw U-20 sink two unarmed merchantmen without warning, heralding the start of unrestricted submarine warfare. This rare image, above, shows the U-20 alongside the accommodation hulk *Waltrante*. After her sinking without warning of merchant ships in January 1915, the submarine U-20 would gain more notoriety when she let loose a single torpedo, which sank the *Lusitania* off the Old Head of Kinsale. The unarmed ocean liner sank in a few minutes with the loss of 1,195 lives. A very short run medal was issued in commemoration in Germany, but was copied in its tens of thousands in Britain.

Remember the *Lusitania*
The sinking of the *Lusitania* coloured
public opinion on both sides of the
Atlantic and the incident became
a rallying point for the recruiting
campaign. *Above:* A recruiting sergeant in
Bermondsey refers to a poster featuring
the ocean liner.

REMEMBER THE LUSITANIA

THE JURY'S VERDICT SAYS:
"We find that the said deceased died from
their prolonged immersion and exhaustion
in the sea eight miles south south-west of
the Old Head of Kinsale on Friday, May 7th,
1915, owing to the sinking of the R.M.S.
Lusitania by a torpedo fired without warning
from a German submarine."

"That this appalling crime was
contrary to international law
and the conventions of all
civilized nations, and we there-
fore charge the officers of the
said submarine, the Emperor
and Government of Germany,
under whose orders they acted,
with the crime of wilful and
wholesale murder before the
tribunal of the civilized world."

*IT IS YOUR DUTY TO TAKE UP THE SWORD OF JUSTICE
TO AVENGE THIS DEVIL'S WORK.*

ENLIST TO-DAY

Right: Under a banner headline,
'Remember the *Lusitania*', this poster
remonstrates against 'this devil's work'.

Italy enters the war

Having proclaimed its neutrality at the outset of the war, Italy announced on 23 May 1915 that it was at war with Austria-Hungary, although not with Germany. The Italian government had been secretly promised substantial territorial gains if it sided with the Allies. Subsequent fighting took place in the mountainous areas of northern Italy, at the Torento and along the Isonzo River towards the port of Trieste. They also came to the help of the Serbians, causing the Austrians to move reinforcements from the Eastern Front to strengthen their own border defences.

Above and top of opposite page: Troops of the Italian Alpine Regiment in 1915, shown with full service kit. As with the Western Front, the Italian Front soon became bogged down in trench warfare, but with the added discomforts of the cold weather and high altitudes.

Bottom opposite page: An Italian artillery column on its way to the front.

British submarines were a constant threat in the Black Sea by mid-1915. The E-7, shown above, sank fifteen vessels on a 24-day patrol in the Sea of Marmara, beginning on 30 June. She was scuttled on 4 September 1915. Below, another British submarine off the Dardanelles.

Opposite: The crew of HMS *Grampus* cheering the submarine E11 on its return from the Dardanelles in July 1915. In three tours of the Sea of Marmara, E11 sank over eighty enemy vessels. Her commander, Martin Nasmith, earned a Victoria Cross for the sub's first tour.

Above: Great Yarmouth in Norfolk was a base for submarines operating in the North Sea. Four submarines are in this view, taken early in 1915. Lowestoft, just along the coast, was the base for destroyers.

Left: A British submarine, seen bow on.

Above: HMS E13 was a British E class submarine built at the Chatham dockyard and commissioned on 9 December 1914. On 14 August 1915 she had been dispatched from Harwich, accompnaied by HMS E8, with orders to sail to the Baltic to attack German shipping. Unfortunately she ran aground in shallow water near the island of Saltholm, which is in the strait that separates Denmark and Sweden, and was attacked by two German torpedo boats – see page 105 – hit repeatledly and set on fire. Having abandoned the submarine fifteen of the crew were killed in the water and the remaineder were only saved by the arrival of a Danish torpedo boat. The incident caused an outrage and the badly damaged submarine was refloated by the Danes, as shown above, and taken to Copenhagen.

Right: HMS *Majestic* sinking in the Dardanelles. Launched at Portsmouth on 31 January 1895, *Majestic* was lost to the submarine U-21 at Cape Helles on 27 May 1915. The Turkish campaign was to see many ships lost to both mines and torpedoes. *Majestic* was the third warship in two weeks to be lost in the campaign. Sinking in nine minutes in only 49 feet of water, it was not until months later that she sank beneath the waves, her masts keeping her above water until one broke and she disappeared.

The American position

Despite the loss of many American citizens in the sinking of the *Lusitania*, US President Dr Woodrow Wilson had to consider conflicting views within the country regarding its stance. The US had declared itself to be neutral, officially at least. There was also an upcoming election in 1916 to consider.

Below: New Yorkers gather in the evenings to watch the latest war bulletins outside the major newspaper buildings.

The President made several offers to mediate between the Allies and the Central Powers, and his primary objective was to keep the US out of the war. Following the sinking of the *Lusitania* Wilson wote a restrained note to the German ambassador protesting about its submarine attacks on shipping. The Germans saw him as a puppet of the British, as shown in this cartoon, right, entitled 'The Dictator', but after the sinking of the White Star liner *Arabic* he threated to cut off diplomatic relations.

(Reproduced by special permission of the Proprietors of "Punch."

BY WAY OF A CHANGE.

Uncle Sam : " Guess I'm about through with letter-writing."

'Nosing' shells by heating them in the furnace and then pressing them into shape. It is an all-male workforce, but this would change as increasing numbers of women take on the work.

JUNE 1915

The Shells Scandal

In the spring of 1915 the British public was shocked to read in the newspapers of a shortage of High Explosive artillery shells on the front line. In particular *The Times* criticised Kitchener, the Secretary of State for War at the time, and control of munitions production was taken out of his hands and a new Ministry of Munitions formed to oversee the large scale production of shells and other munitions. The Munitions of War Act of 1915 brought private companies under the ministry's control and regulated wages, hours and working conditions. *Above:* A stock of shells at a British factory, 'ready for dispatch'.

Above: Scottish women at work in a munitions factory. The work could be arduous, and it was often highly dangerous handling the chemicals which filled the shells. There was also the ever present risk of an accident. *Below:* Molten metal being poured into moulds at the foundry.

Above: A line up showing the sixteen different types of shells used by the French Army.

Right: Inside the massive Krupps gun works in Germany, showing the Sheffield-made heavy machinery. Based in Essen, Krupps produced most of the artillery for the German Army, including its massive the Big Bertha type of siege gun. Friedrich Krupp Germaniawerft, in Kiel, also constructed warships and submarines for the Imperial Navy.

THE SOLDIER AND THE MUNITION-WORKER.
"WE'RE BOTH NEEDED TO SERVE THE GUNS!"
[*With acknowledgments to a popular poster.*]

'We're both needed to serve the guns,' states the poster, top. It provided the inspiration for this *Punch* cartoon published in June 1915, with the design adapted to reflect the nation's gratitude to the Munitions Minister, Lloyd George, following the debacle of the Shell Scandal.

Above: Despite the war, and the demands on increased production, some aspects of normal life continued as usual, including industrial action by the miners. This photograph shows men leaving the mines during the South Wales strike.

BACK THEM UP

MY DUTY

INVEST IN THE
WAR LOAN

Right: Doing your duty on the Home Front meant dipping your hand into your pocket to feed the war economy through the War Loan and National Bonds schemes. This poster was published by the Parliamentary War Savings Committee in July 1915.

The Zeppelin killer: Poster depicting Warneford, although he is not mentioned by name.

Warneford's Zeppelin

In January 1915 the Kaiser had reluctantly given permission for raids on England, but stipulated that they were to be against military targets and that London was to be excluded. Following the raids on the Norfolk coast in January, when two airships targeting the Humber were blown off course, the bombing of London's docks was authorised in the following month. On 31 May 1915 the LZ 38 made the first raid on London, dropping 120 bombs on the capital. What the British needed was a victory against the raiders.

This came on 15 June 1915 when Reginald Warneford of the Royal Naval Air Service, shown opposite, flying in a Morane-Saulnier monoplane, brought down the LZ 37 near Ghent. Warneford was awarded the VC for his actions, but they were eclipsed in September 1916 when Captain William Leefe Robinson downed the Shutte-Lanz airship, SL 11, over Cuffley in Hertfordshire, shown right.

The Isonzo Campaign on the Italian Front
Wounded at the field hospital after the First Battle of Isonzo which began on 23 June 1915, between the armies of Italy and Austria. The aim of the Italians had been to drive the Austrians away from defensive positions. Over the next two years there were eleven battles here.

Mines

Above: The laying of mines was a relatively safe job, providing you weren't caught. The removal was another matter. This mine has been defused but would you hammer away at a live mine? One of the German crew here is obviously braver than we would be.

Left: A German mine seen close up. The Germans could lay mines from converted merchant ships and destroyers, and latterly from specially designed submarines.

German torpedo boats

These were used for fast incursions into enemy territory or close to the enemy fleet. These small, manoeuvrable craft were extremely fast with speeds of up to 40 knots. The German torpedo boats had less opportunity to sink enemy vessels but British and Italian torpedo boats in the Mediterranean sank many enemy ships.

Right: A torpedo explodes. Britain had torpedo factories in Greenock and in Portland, making Whitehead torpedoes for the navy.

Lord Kitchener, the poster boy of the First World War, although in recent years there has been some dispute concerning whether Alfred Leete's design for *London Opinion* actually appeared as a recruiting poster.

JULY 1915

Above: Cigarettes being distributed to the men of Princess Patricia's Canadian Light Infantry, in camp on Salisbury Plain.

Kitchener's men

Lord Kitchener oversaw the raising of many battalions of Pals Regiments, which were in training by summer 1915. Using the tactic of encouraging you to join up with friends, workmates and family, the concentrating of so many from the same town in one battalion would cause huge problems when these regiments had been trained and entered the fight against the Germans. Kitchener would not live to see the devastation the first days of the Battle of the Somme caused in many British towns and cities, with whole streets of men wiped out in the conflict.

Below: Kitchener inspecting troops at the Guildhall in London, 1915.

Above: Kitchener addresses an enthusiastic crowd outside London's Guildhall after a recruiting speech calling for 'yet more men'. Many of these came from the dominions and, below, the High Commissioner for Australia is seen inspecting a contingent of his countrymen.

Into 1915 all corners of the Empire continued to rally to the flag. *Above:* Farewell march of Canada's second contingent through the streets of Montreal. *Below:* Winnipeg rifles crossing a bridge over the Jaques Cartier river, testing the work of the Canadian Engineering Corps.

Scuttling the Königsberg

SMS *Königsberg* was a German light cruiser built in 1905. At the start of the war, she was in East Africa and sank HMS *Pegasus* at Zanzibar in September 1914. After a long search, she was discovered in the Rufuji delta and eventually scuttled on 11 July 1915.

The forecastle of HMS *Iron Duke*, which was named after the Duke of Wellington. *Iron Duke* was commissioned in 1914 and saw little action till Jutland, missing out on the Battle of Dogger Bank. She was the First Battle Fleet flagship until 1917.

Supplies

The supply chain maintained the life blood of the forces fighting at the Front, not only by supplying the prodigious quantities of shells and bullets, but also the food for both men and their horses, as well as clothing, medicines and other essentials. These images show the Army Service Corps at work, bringing water and foodstuff for the troops.

Where the roads were good enough motor vehicles could be used very effectively, but on poorer terrain nearer to the Front only the horses would get through. *Above:* British vehicles were often commandeered private cars and trucks. These are in France. *Below:* A very basic armoured gun position has been added at the back of this Turkish car.

Above: A German transport column outside Nisch. Both sides made extensive use of horses to transport the goods and the guns. It has been estimated that in total around six million horses took part in the war, and a million died on the British side alone. To meet the demand a special breeding programme was instigated and thousands of horses were confiscated from civilians. In general they were well treated, and the Blue Cross Fund was established to care for wounded horses at the front. A Blue Cross receiving depot in France is shown below.

Above: Red Cross ambulance dogs were used by both sides during the war. Specially trained, these canine heroes could take bandages and painkillers to soldiers trapped in No Man's Land.

Above: Trained German Shepherd dogs used as Red Cross dogs at the front. Below is an elephant from Carl Hackenback's circus used for heavy haulage. With many hundreds of thousands of horses taken up for the war effort, elephants were used by both sides in place of horses and there are examples of them being used for farming work in Britain.

Illustration of a British mobile anti-aircraft gun in action on the Western Front in 1915.

AUGUST 1915

Above: The Kaiser presenting Iron Crosses to a group of German aviators.

The major technical innovation of the war for the fighter pilot was developed by Fokker, who invented a means of firing through a spinning propeller blade without damaging the blade. His interrupter gear was eventually used by both sides and its invention changed the design of fighter aircraft, leading to the single-seat fighter we know so well today.

Above: Attaching a bomb to a German aircraft. In the early stages of the war the aircraft could only carry small bombs, and the method of aiming them was very elementary. It was only later, from 1917 onwards, that Germany had aircraft such as the Gotha G and the Zeppelin-Staaken R.VI, which were big enough to carry heavier bombloads and undertake strategic bombing raids over greater distances.

Above: Printed in a British publication in 1915, the caption for this photograph describes the German emperor as the 'War-worn Kaiser'. One year into the conflict, Kaiser 'Bill' was the natural target for ridicule in the British press and his upturned moustache made him instantly recognisable in countless cartoon appearances.

Right: Crown Prince Wilhelm, the eldest son of Kaiser Wilhelm II, was the last Crown Prince of the Kingdom of Prussia and the German Empire. In August 1914 he was named commander of the 5th Army, despite his inexperience in military matters, and from 1915 onwards he also held the role of commander of the Army Group Crown Prince.

Right: Although Kaiser Wilhelm retained ultimate authority, it was Field Marshall Paul von Hindenburg who held the reigns and as the war progressed, Germany in effect had become a military dictatorship.

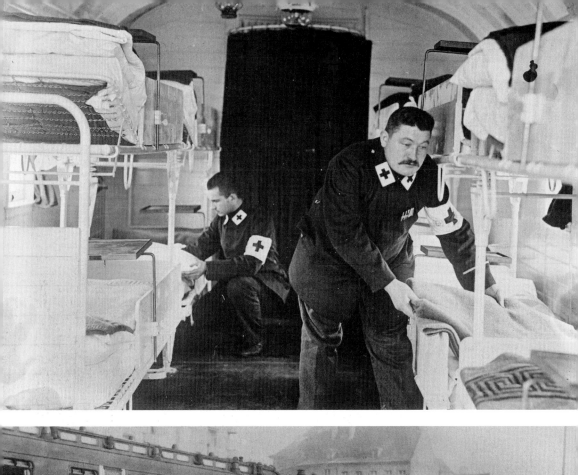

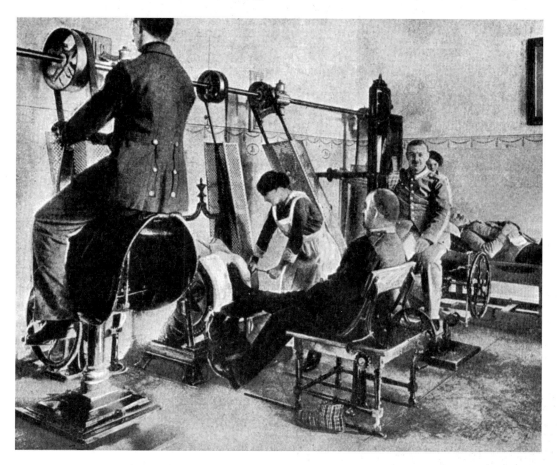

Wounded soldiers in Berlin

Above: German soldiers undergoing 'scientific' treatment in a Berlin military hospital. The machines are designed to build up their strength. Note the saddle-like contraption on the left, presumably for recovering cavalrymen. Ensuring the well-being of the injured was important. After all, they could return to fight again, hence the huge efforts that went into recuperating them as quickly as possible.

Railways were hugely important during the war not just for the movement of men and materiel but also for the removal of the wounded back behind the lines. Special hospital or ambulance trains were built by both sides.

Opposite: A German Hospital train in Berlin. In the upper image the orderlies prepare beds for the wounded, and, below, the Kaiserin talks to wounded soldiers who arrived on the train, and to the nurses who will be taking care of them.

German war workers
These women are being trained to drive Berlin's trams. Just as in the UK, the drain on manpower meant that more and more women needed to take up previously male dominated jobs, both in the factories and in public services such as transportation.

Eastern Front

Above: German pioneers repairing the Vistula bridge between Praga and Warsaw.

Right: Map of the country to the east of the Warta, showing the relative positions of Warsaw, Ivangorod and Cracow. The black lines show the approximate position of the Germans, and the shaded lines the Russian, at the time when Hindeburg's army made its failed attempt to seize the Polish capital. On 18 September 1915 they captured Vilna.

They called it the 'March of the Millions'
Top: Russian troops on the way to Cracow, the second largest city in Poland, which they had beseiged in November 1914. *Middle:* Russian infantry forming up outside a village in readiness for an advance. *Bottom:* New Russian troops en route to the Warsaw battle-line.

Above: Following the capture of Novo Georgievski, the Germans take posession of the citadel.

Below: German engineers at work on repairing the damaged bridge at Lemberg.

Above: The spoils of war. German troops examine a pair of captured Russian machine guns.

Below: The wounded disembarking from a special train at Allenstein in Eastern Prussia.

The Russians had taken a pounding on the Eastern Front and in a few months they have been pushed out of Galicia and Poland. On 21 August 1915, Tzar Nicholas took personal command of the Russian Army. He is shown above, greeting his officers in the field.

Right: The corpses of several Russian soldiers who had become entangled trying to force their way through the enemy's barbed wire.

Above: Before battle, a communion service takes place for the Russian soldiers.

Below: With their rifles held in salute, the men of the Russian Fongorijski Regiment give three cheers for their British allies and for King George.

SEPTEMBER 1915

Second Battle of Champagne
Above: A troop of Uhlans, Light Cavalry, leaving cover in the Champagne district to charge the French. In fact the Second Battle of Champagne was a French offensive against the Germans, beginning on 25 September 1915 and continuing into early November. The German defensive line was broken in four places and 14,000 prisoners and several guns were captured. However, a German counter-attack on 29 September recaptured the ground. By its consclusion the French had lost 145,000 men and the Germans 72,500.

Following on from the experience of the Second Battle of Champagne, the Allies put greater emphasis on its artillery to smash the enemy's entrenched positions. A French field gun is shown above, and, below, a larger 15.5-cm gun within its camouflaged emplacement.

Prisoners of War

The First World War saw the capture of enemy personnel on an unprecedented scale and by the end of the conflict about 8 million men had been taken prisoner for the duration. The German Empire held around 2.5 million prisoners of war, Russia had 2.9 million, and between them France and Britain held about 720,000 men. Ironically, despite the often harsh treatment of prisoners, even though all nations had pledged to follow the Hague rules on their fair treatment, the POWs had a much higher survival rate than the men still fighting at the front.

Top image: British prisoners being marched to a camp at Doberitz, about twenty miles away from Berlin. *Bottom:* A mix of French and British officers also in German hands.

Prison guards at Doberitz are shown censoring the prisoners' mail, above, to ensure that sensitive information doesn't get through. While below, British and French prisoners sort the mail, presumably incoming. Despite the staged photographs there were some reports of harsh treatment of the prisonors by their guards. Conditions were far worse in the Russia prison camps and starvation was not uncommon and around one-quarter of its POWS died in captivity.

Two images of British prisoners being held in a camp in Germany, with bread being handed out at meal time.

More scenes from the German prison camps. It is smiles all round for the camera, above. Below, French prisoners are shown receiving a delivery of cabbages at a camp at Wunsdorf, Zossen, to the south of Berlin.

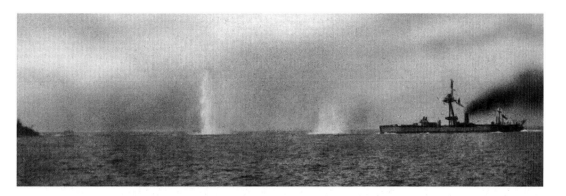

British monitors bombarding the Belgian coast

Once the Germans had occupied Belgium, the monitors shelled the coastal defences and army camps inland. With their low freeboard and shallow draught, they made poor sea boats. *Above:* Unnamed, this is probably one of the Lord Clive class of monitors. In 1918, *Lord Clive* was fitted with a single 18-in gun, which only fired four shots in anger before the end of the war. *Below:* HMS *Terror* was an Erebus-class monitor, laid down at Harland & Wolff's in Govan in 1915. She spent her war career bombarding Belgium and was damaged by a torpedo from a German torpedo boat on 19 October 1917. Her service speed was 12 knots and she was armed with two 15-in guns. She was sunk off Libya in 1941.

Above: Commissioned in August 1915, HMS *Marshall Soult* was equipped with twin 15-in guns and was designed to bombard Belgium from the sandbanks around Zeebrugge and Ostend. With twin screws, she was fitted with two diesel engines and had a maximum speed of 9 knots.

OCTOBER 1915

Serbia

Above: Serbian gunners left dead at their posts on the battlefield after clashes with Austrian forces near Belgrade. Austria-Hungary had declared war on Serbia following the assasination of Archduke Ferdinand in August 1914 by Gavrilo Princip, a member of the Young Bosnia organisation. The Serbian forces had enjoyed initial successes, but were eventually overpowered by the Central Powers in 1915. On 9 October Austro-Hungarian troops occupied Belgrade, and on 14 October Serbia and Bulgaria had declared war against each other, leaving landlocked Serbia beseiged from all sides.

Austrian machine gunners in action in the snow, above, and Austrian prisoners arriving at Nish, below. When Belgrade was bombed the Serbians made Nish their temporary capital.

Neuve-Chapelle
The British launched a limted offensive at Neuve-Chapelle in Artois, north-eastern France, on
10 March 1915. British and Indian forces made good progress until German counterattacks
halted their advance. They dug in but under heavy bombardment suffered more than 11,500
casualties. They learned the hard way that in future artillery fire was the only way to break
through the trenches. This famous poster is by the celebrated Welsh artist Frank Brangwyn.

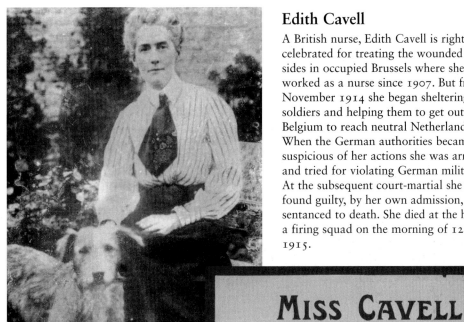

Edith Cavell

A British nurse, Edith Cavell is rightly celebrated for treating the wounded of both sides in occupied Brussels where she had worked as a nurse since 1907. But from November 1914 she began sheltering British soldiers and helping them to get out of Belgium to reach neutral Netherlands. When the German authorities became suspicious of her actions she was arrested and tried for violating German military law. At the subsequent court-martial she was found guilty, by her own admission, and was sentanced to death. She died at the hands of a firing squad on the morning of 12 October 1915.

Above: Nurse Cavell photographed before the war with one of her dogs in her Brussels' garden. After the war, her body was reinterred in Norwich Cathedral after a state funeral at Westminster Abbey.

Right: This postcard, commemorating the death of Edith Cavell, was printed in Paris.

Dazzle paint

From the largest to the smallest merchant ship, many served their country. *Inset:* The North Sea cargo vessel *Chesterfield* is seen in dazzle paint. Dazzle paint was invented by Norman Wilkinson. He surmised that you could not hide a ship at sea but that you could confuse a submariner if he could not work out the size, speed and direction of travel of a ship. *Main picture:* HMT *Olympic*, once a White Star liner, spent part of 1916 trooping to Mudros, and to Canada to bring troops over to Europe. Laid up for a while in 1916, at the end of the Dardanelles campaign, she also spent 1917 and 1918 trooping. She is the only large ocean liner to sink a submarine.

NOVEMBER 1915

The spectre of a Zeppelin hangs over the familiar landmarks of London. The airship raids were intended to provoke panic among the British, especially within the civilian population, but despite the many casualties and the damage caused, the Kaiser's vision of Londoners fleeing from the capital did not materialise. This illustration is from a British recruiting poster as the Zeppelin manace proved to be a powerful symbol of the threat to the homeland.

PUNCH, OR THE LONDON CHARIVARI.—October 27, 1915.

OUR FRIEND THE ENEMY.

John Bull (*very calmly*). "AH, HERE HE COMES AGAIN—MY BEST RECRUITER."

Zeppelin bombs

In addition to explosive bombs, the Zeppelins also dropped incendiary bombs that contained white phosphorus and thermite to generate fierce flames that burned at extremely high temperatures. Fortunately some of these could be neutralised if smothered with sand and soil, and photographs of the bombs were published to aid recognition. These images come from *The Sphere*, June 1915. *Upper right:* A policeman is holding up a neutralised bomb and, to the left, the remains of one that had burnt itself out.

Opposite page: A *Punch* cartoon, 27 October 1915.

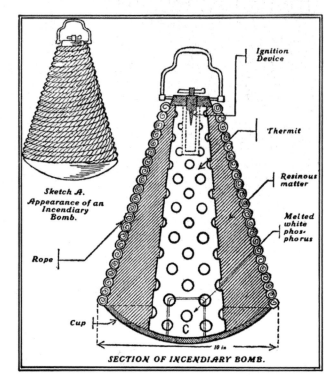

Sketch A.
Appearance of an Incendiary Bomb.

Rope

Cup

Ignition Device

Thermit

Resinous matter

Melted white phosphorus

10 in

SECTION OF INCENDIARY BOMB.

THE RAIDER.
PUBLICATION SANCTIONED BY OFFICIAL PRESS BUREAU
Publishing Office
39, St. Andrew's Hill, E.C.　　　　　(Copyright)

One example from several similar series of popular postcards depicting the Zeppelin raiders. These would often feature a number of cards telling the story of the raider being spotted and then brought down in flames. One series began with 'The Low Down Thing' and concluded with 'The Low Down Thing Brought Down Low'. Other cards depicted podgy Zeppelins with the face of the Kaiser, his great moustache formed by the flames of the falling airship. More gruesome cards featured real photographs of the wrecks, including some extraordinarily graphic images of the the dead Zeppelin crewmen. As the war progressed, and the British defences improved, particularly in terms of the newest fighter aircraft, the Zeppelins proved to be increasingly vulnerable.

BUCHANAN'S
SCOTCH WHISKIES

STUDY IN BLACK AND WHITE: DESTROYER SIGHTING ZEPPELIN.

"RED SEAL"
48/- per doz.

"ROYAL HOUSEHOLD"
(An Extra Special Blend of Choice Old Whiskies.)
60/- per doz.

"BLACK & WHITE"
54/- per doz.

James Buchanan & Co., Ltd., with their subsidiary companies, hold the largest Stocks of Whisky maturing in Bond in Scotland, and are thus able to guarantee the continued superior excellence of their brands.

At first sight an unlikely subject for an advertisement for whisky.

WAR ECONOMY.

Lady Sybil de Vere. "Do look at those extraordinary people. Their clothes are quite new!"
Sir Hugo. "Rotten bad form!"

Above: Punch cartoon published in November 1915.

Home Front economies

The National Committee for War Savings made appeals against extravagance in women's dress. 'To dress extravagently in wartime is worse than bad form, it is unpatriotic.' The *Punch* cartoon reveals the effect of the war economy on some, and reinforcing peer pressure was part of the wider propaganda campaign to influence the public's behaviour in a way that had never been seen before.

BAD FORM IN DRESS.

The National Organizing Committee for War Savings appeals against extravagance in women's dress.

Many women have already recognized that elaboration and variety in dress are bad form in the present crisis, but there is still a large section of the community, both amongst the rich and amongst the less well-to-do, who appear to make little or no difference in their habits.

New clothes should only be bought when absolutely necessary, and these should be durable and suitable for all occasions. Luxurious forms, for example, of hats, boots, shoes, stockings, gloves, and veils should be avoided.

It is essential, not only that money should be saved, but that labour employed in the clothing trades should be set free.

Left: 'Bad Form in Dress.' A wartime poster extolling the importance of saving money in all areas of everyday life.

No. 118.—Child's White Linen Coat, embroidered brown, saxe blue, cherry, and mauve. 18 in. long, for child about two years. Price 24/6 each.

Larger sizes can also be made to order.

We make a speciality of Layettes from 10 guineas which we can execute very quickly.

Baby Linen Department. — No. 117. — Little Boy's Suit, with knickers of linen and muslin blouse smocked with colour to match knickers. Colours: cherry, pale blue, saxe blue, brown, mauve, and all white with sky smocking, and white with pink smocking, and size to fit child of 2-3 years. Price 17/9

No. 121.—Little Girl's White Linen Coat, embroidered blue, 20 inches long, 25/6, 22 inches long, 27/6. Can be had in sherry, saxe, mauve, brown, and light blue, with white collar and cuffs, white linen hat to match under-lined colour to match coat. Price 10/6

No. 118. No. 117.

Robinson & Cleaver Ltd.
The Linen Hall,
Regent Street, London.W.

Every Genuine Burberry Garment bears the Burberry Label.

Burberry Gown
A perfect example of all that a tailored gown should be. Its simple design serves to accentuate its elegance and distinction.

Discrimination and Good Taste
are vindicated by the selection of
BURBERRY
Weatherproof Dress
because it is the most satisfactory form of protection available, when viewed from the standpoints of Efficiency, Distinction and Economy.

EFFICIENCY is attained by Burberry Weave-Proof—which provides faultless weather-resistance—in conjunction with practical design and expert craftsmanship.

DISTINCTION is assured by simple and artistic models, aided by exceptional variety of materials of most alluring colourings and original patterns.

ECONOMY is observed in the fact that BURBERRY remains in vogue long after the fashion of its date has become *démodée*.

Write for patterns of newest Materials, together with illustrated Book of Models.

COATS AND GOWNS CLEANED by Burberrys are returned practically as good as new. Price List on application.

BURBERRYS
HAYMARKET LONDON
8 & 10 Boul. Malesherbes PARIS
Basingstoke and Provincial Agents

In some quarters there was a sense of unease that for the rich the war made little or no difference to their lifestyle. The poster campaign cited three ways to help the war effort: Reduce petrol consumption, don't buy new clothes and, of course, don't keep more servants than you really need. "In this way you will save money for the War, set the right example, and free labour for more useful purposes.' Another poster suggested that such excessive consumption coule be helping the Germans.

It was all well and good in theory, but businesses had to keep going too and as the advertisements which appear at the top of this page demonstrate, the goods were still available if you could afford them. They come from the pages of *The Graphic* magazine.

Right: Another of the posters designed to encourage a less ostentatious lifestyle in wartime.

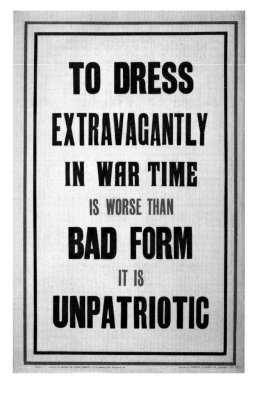

TO DRESS EXTRAVAGANTLY IN WAR TIME IS WORSE THAN **BAD FORM** IT IS **UNPATRIOTIC**

H.M.S. CARMANIA
(ROYAL S.)
BOYS
OF THE
OLD
BRIGADE
RATS

Laconia's

Above: Another Cunard liner which was heavily involved in the war effort was HMS *Carmania*. Converted to an armed merchant cruiser, this view shows some of her stokers and firemen, complete with ship's cat. They have come up on the deck for some much-needed fresh air. During 1915, she patrolled the coast of Portugal and Spain to prevent enemy ships entering the Mediterranean.

Left: At the start of the First World War, Cunard's *Laconia* was refitted as an armed merchant cruiser and based at Simonstown, South Africa. She patrolled the South Atlantic and Indian Ocean until April 1915. She was returned to Cunard in 1916 and was sunk by torpedo from U-50 on 25 February 1917 with the loss of twelve people off Fastnet. Crewmembers are shown here, photographed in decidely non-standard dress.

Lazarett-Schiff.

Hospital ships

Used to transfer casualties from the Eastern Front back to Germany, the North German Lloyd steamer SS *Schleswig* was converted into a hospital ship in 1915 and is shown here at Danzig. Built in 1902 at Stettin, she was given to the French as war reparation in 1919 and operated by Messageries Maritime as *General Duchesne*. *Below:* When the Italians entered the war on the side of the Allies, their navy and naval bases helped greatly in the efforts against the Austro-Hungarians and in the supply chain of the Dardanelles campaign. The HMHS *Re D'Italia* was a Lloyd Sabuado ship built in 1906. During 1915, she was used as a hospital ship, taking wounded soldiers between Italy and Malta.

Nave Ospedale "Re d' Italia,,

12

Launched in February 1914, the White Star liner SS *Britannic*, Britain's largest ship, lay uncompleted in Belfast until 1915, when work began on her to convert her to a hospital ship. She had been starved of materials, which had been diverted elsewhere for the war effort, but the demands of the Gallipoli campaign saw a need for both hospital and troopships. As G608, she is shown here at Southampton Docks while being coaled.

DECEMBER 1915

In the early days of the war, tetanus took the lives of thousands of men when their battle wounds became infected in the intensively cultivated soil of the Western Front. It was an excruciatingly painful way to die, and this is Dutch artist Louis Raemaekers' depiction of a tetanus ward. An effective vaccine was not developed until 1924.

After the hiatus of 1914's Christmas truce, which saw the playing of football between adversaries in No Man's Land, subsequent celebrations were more subdued as the combatants settled down for the long haul. *Above and below:* Two scenes of German celebrations, behind the lines, above, and wounded soldiers in a hospital ward in Berlin, below.

Minesweeper
Designed and built for the North British Railway, but requisitioned by the Royal Navy, the paddle steamer *Fair Maid* was launched in December 1915. Her career was rather short, as this paddle minesweeper sank near Cross Sands Buoy in November 1916. Mine sweeping was a dangerous business and many minesweepers were lost to the weapons they were designed to recover.

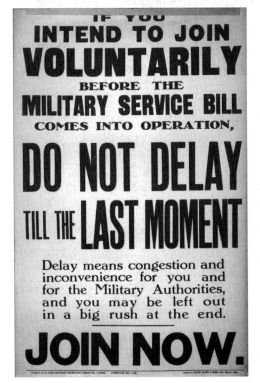

Conscription

The British recruiting posters from the first year of the war were often presented as a friendly appeal from your pals. One poster stated; 'Why not join the army? You will like it. Your pals will like.' It was about playing the game, which in this case, shown left, was a game of cards. But the war's appetite was insatiable and voluntary service was not enough and it would finish when the Military Service Bill was passed in January 1916 and came into effect in the spring.

Left: Recruiting poster issued in late 1915 advising men eligible for military service to join voluntarily before the introduction of conscription in the new year. Avoiding 'congestion and inconvenience' does not seem much of an incentive for those who, by this stage, had not already chosen to join up as volunteers.

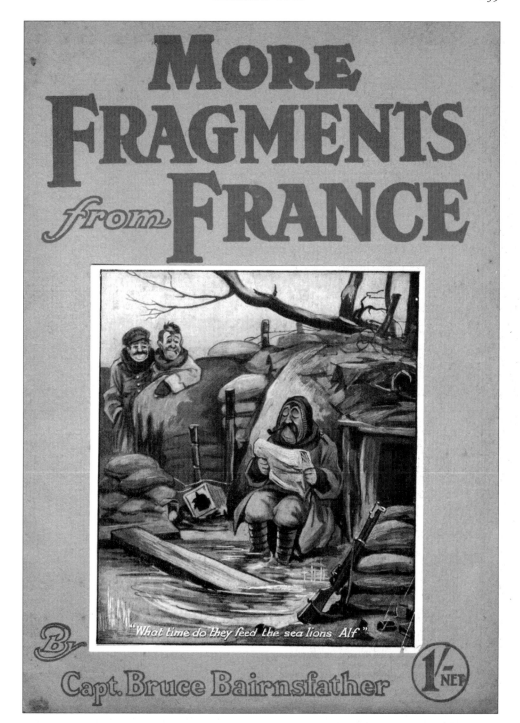

Fragments From France
The Old Bill character was created by Captain (Charles) Bruce Bairnsfather, who had served in a machine gun unit of the Royal Warwickshire Regiment but was sent back to Blighty in 1915 suffering from shellshock and hearing loss sustained in the Second Battle of Ypres.

A wartime advertisement from the 'age of petrol'. British companies were not reticent in linking their products with the war effort, no matter how tenuous the link. This advert appeared in *The Great War*, a weekly serialised part-work history of the war published from 1914 onwards as the cevents took place.